READING POWER

19th Century American Inventors

The Inventions of

Martha Coston

Signal Flares That Saved Sailors' Lives

Holly Cefrey

The Rosen Publishing Group's
PowerKids Press™
New York

Published in 2003 by The Rosen Publishing Group, Inc.
29 East 21st Street, New York, NY 10010

First Edition

Book Design: Daniel Hosek

Photo Credits: Cover, pp. 6 (inset), 14 (foreground), 15, 20 Science, Industry, and Business Library, New York Public Library, Astor, Lenox, and Tilden Foundations; pp. 4–5 Independence National Historic Park; pp. 6–7, 8–9, 17 Library of Congress, Prints and Photographs Division; p. 10–11 © Burstein Collection/Corbis; p. 13 © Hulton/Archive/Getty Images; pp. 14 (background), 21 United States Patent and Trademark Office; p. 16 courtesy of U.S. Naval Historical Center; p. 18–19 © Corbis

Library of Congress Cataloging-in-Publication Data

Cefrey, Holly.
The inventions of Martha Coston : signal flares that saved sailors'
lives / Holly Cefrey.
 p. cm. — (19th century American inventors)
Includes bibliographical references and index.
Summary: Chronicles the work of Martha Coston to perfect and market
signal flares to the U.S. Navy and abroad.
ISBN 0-8239-6444-2
1. Coston, Martha J., 1826-1886—Juvenile literature. 2. Coston,
Benjamin Franklin, 1821-1848—Juvenile literature. 3. Inventors—United
States—Biography—Juvenile literature. 4. Flares—Juvenile literature.
5. Signals and signaling—Juvenile literature. [1. Coston, Martha J.,
1826-1886. 2. Signals and signaling. 3. Inventors. 4.
Women—Biography.] I. Title. II. Series.
VK140.C674 C44 2003
623.89'4—dc21

2002001797

Contents

In the Beginning

Martha Hunt was born in Baltimore, Maryland, in 1826. When Martha was very young, her father died. After her father died, Martha's mother moved the family to Philadelphia, Pennsylvania, because the schools there were good.

The Fact Box

As a child, Martha was called Sunbeam by her mother.

Philadelphia, Pennsylvania, 1830s

In 1840, Martha met Benjamin Franklin Coston. Benjamin Coston became a close friend of the family. He helped Martha with her school lessons.

Martha Coston

Philadelphia, Pennsylvania, 1840s

7

In 1842, Benjamin Coston worked as a scientist and inventor for the United States Navy. His lab was at the Washington Navy Yard in Washington, D.C. In the same year, Coston and Martha Hunt got married.

In 1846, Benjamin Coston left the navy and moved with his wife and their children to Boston, Massachusetts.

Benjamin Coston worked at the Washington Navy Yard (shown here). He invented a submarine that could stay underwater for eight hours without coming up.

The Signal Flare

In 1847, Benjamin Coston became sick and died. Martha Coston and her children moved back to Philadelphia to live with her mother. There, she found some notes for a new invention that her husband had started but never tested. The invention was a signal flare.

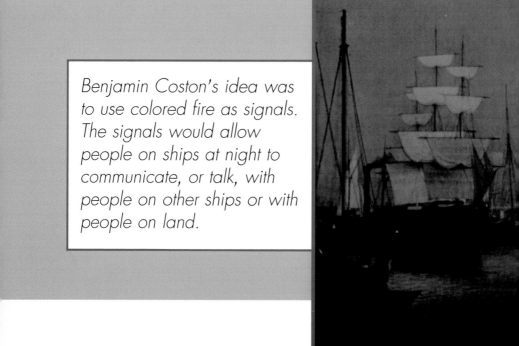

Benjamin Coston's idea was to use colored fire as signals. The signals would allow people on ships at night to communicate, or talk, with people on other ships or with people on land.

Benjamin Coston had made a few signal flares and had given them to the navy. After his death, the navy tested the flares and found that they did not work. Martha Coston wrote to some navy officers and said she wanted to continue her husband's work. A navy official told Martha Coston to keep on working to find a way to make the flares work.

Isaac Toucey was the navy official who told Martha to continue her work on the signal flares.

Martha Coston got the idea of using fireworks in the flare. She hired scientists and a fireworks maker to help her make the signal flare. By 1859, she succeeded in getting the flares to work.

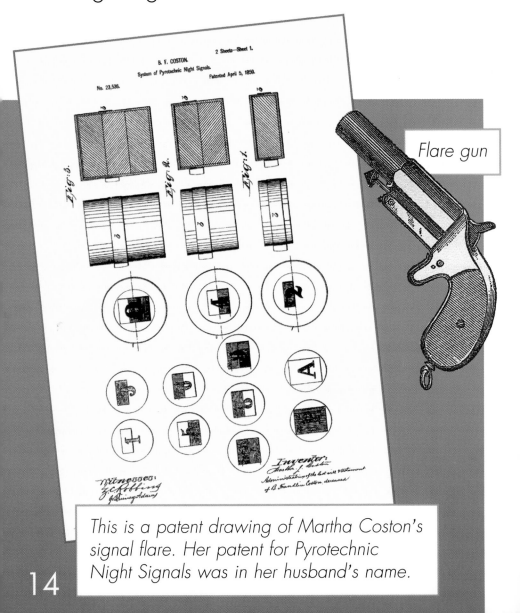

Flare gun

This is a patent drawing of Martha Coston's signal flare. Her patent for Pyrotechnic Night Signals was in her husband's name.

Martha Coston's new signal flares were bright and colorful. They stayed in the sky longer than before so that they could be seen easily. At night, the flares could be seen from 15 to 20 miles away.

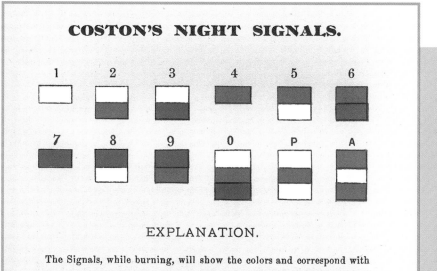

The signal flares needed to have simple color combinations and be easy to use. The light given off by a flare had to be bright and long lasting. The colors of Coston's signal flares were red, white, and green.

Going into Business

The navy wanted to use Coston's flares. They bought her patent for the flares for $20,000. The navy also asked Martha Coston to make the flares for them. She set up the Coston Supply Company to make signal flares.

U.S. Navy ships, 1861

"The signals by night are very much more useful than the signals by day made with flags, for at night the signals can be so plainly read that mistakes are impossible. . . ."
—Admiral David D. Porter of the U.S. Navy, in a letter to Martha Coston

Saving Lives

During the Civil War, the Northern armies used the Coston Signal Flares. The flares were used to let the soldiers know when other Northern soldiers were in danger. The flares were also used to send messages.

On December 30, 1862, the U.S. Navy ship, the Monitor, was caught in a bad storm at sea. As the ship began to sink, the sailors lit Coston's flares. Another ship saw the flares and came to save the sailors.

Martha Coston traveled all over the world selling the signal flares. She sold the flares in France, Holland, Italy, and other countries. Over the years, her invention has saved thousands of lives. Her signal flares are still used today.

In 1886, Martha Coston wrote a book about her life called A Signal Success.

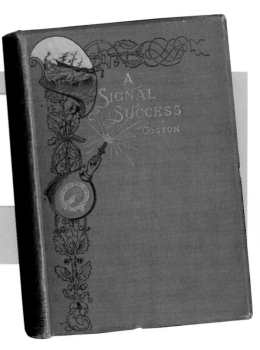

Time Line

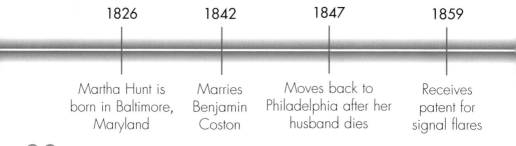

1826	1842	1847	1859
Martha Hunt is born in Baltimore, Maryland	Marries Benjamin Coston	Moves back to Philadelphia after her husband dies	Receives patent for signal flares

Martha Coston continued to make her flare better. In 1871, she received a patent for a twist-igniting device, a special tool that made it easier to start the flare burning.

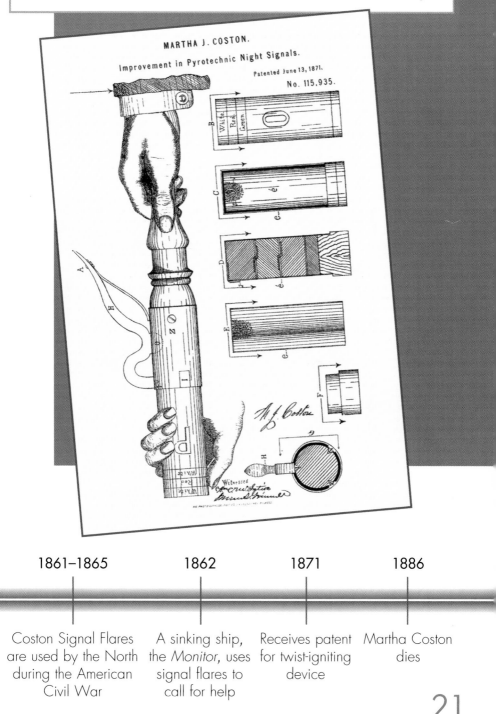

1861–1865	1862	1871	1886
Coston Signal Flares are used by the North during the American Civil War	A sinking ship, the *Monitor*, uses signal flares to call for help	Receives patent for twist-igniting device	Martha Coston dies

Glossary

Civil War (**sihv**-uhl **wor**) the war fought from 1861 to 1885 between the southern and northern parts of the United States

device (dih-**vys**) something invented for a special purpose or use

invention (ihn-**vehn**-shuhn) something new that someone thinks of or makes

inventor (ihn-**vehn**-tuhr) a person who thinks of or makes something new

lab (**lab**) a room or building with special equipment where scientists do tests and experiments

official (uh-**fihsh**-uhl) someone who holds an important government job

patent (**pat**-nt) a legal paper that gives an inventor the right to make or sell his or her invention

pyrotechnic (py-ruh-**tehk**-nihk) having to do with fireworks

scientist (**sy**-uhn-tihst) a person who studies the world by viewing it and using tests

signal flare (**sihg**-nuhl flair) a tool that makes a burst of fireworks to get attention

Resources

Books

Women Inventors & Their Discoveries
by Ethlie Ann Vare and Greg Ptacek
Oliver Press (1993)

*Girls Think of Everything: Stories of
Ingenious Inventions by Women*
by Catherine Thimmesh
Houghton Mifflin Company (2000)

Web Sites

Due to the changing nature of Internet links, PowerKids
Press has developed an online list of Web sites related
to the subjects of this book. This site is updated regularly.
Please use this link to access the list:

http://www.powerkidslinks.com/ncai/imc/

Index

C
Civil War, 18, 21
Coston, Benjamin, 6,
   8–10, 12, 20

F
fireworks, 14

I
invention, 10, 20
inventor, 8

L
lab, 8

O
official, 12–13

P
patent, 14, 16, 20–21

S
scientist, 8, 14
signal flare, 10,
   12–16, 20–21

Word Count: 418

Note to Librarians, Teachers, and Parents

If reading is a challenge, Reading Power is a solution! Reading Power is perfect for readers who want high-interest subject matter at an accessible reading level. These fact-filled, photo-illustrated books are designed for readers who want straightforward vocabulary, engaging topics, and a manageable reading experience. With clear picture/text correspondence, leveled Reading Power books put the reader in charge. Now readers have the power to get the information they want and the skills they need in a user-friendly format.